The Intelligent Social Change Journey

[Foundation for the *Possibilities that are YOU!* series]

by

Alex Bennet, David Bennet, Arthur Shelley,
Theresa Bullard and John Lewis

An imprint of **MQIPress** (2018)
Frost, West Virginia
ISBN 978-1-949829-23-5

MQIPress

Frost, West Virginia
303 Mountain Quest Lane, Marlinton, WV 24954
United States of America
Telephone: 304-799-7267
eMail: alex@mountainquestinstitute.com
www.mountainquestinstitute.com
www.mountainquestinn.com
www.MQIPress.com
www.Myst-Art.com

ISBN 978-1-949829-23-5
Graphics by Fleur Flohil
Cover Art by Cindy Taylor

The Intelligent Social Change Journey (ISCJ) is a developmental journey of the body, mind and heart, moving from the heaviness of cause-and-effect linear extrapolations, to the fluidity of co-evolving with our environment, to the lightness of breathing our thought and feelings into reality.

Preface

Never in the history of humanity has the *opportunity for and need to change* so clearly manifested itself into our everyday existence. While the potential for catastrophic destruction has loomed over us since the mid-20th century, we are still here, admittedly a world in turmoil on many fronts—plagued with economic, political, eco-system, social, cultural, religious and political fragmentation—but also a humanity that is awakening to our true potential and power. Just learning how to co-evolve with an increasingly changing, uncertain and complex external environment, we are now beginning to recognize that it is the change available *within* our internal environment *and* energetic connections to each other and the larger whole that offer up an invitation to an *incluessent future*, that state of Being far beyond the small drop of previous possibility accepted as true, far beyond that which we have known to dream.[1]

The Intelligent Social Change Journey (ISCJ), which is at the core of the five parts of *The Profundity and Bifurcation of Change* (PBC) and the 22 little books that are the Conscious Look Book series *Possibilities that are YOU!* (PY), is a developmental journey of the body, mind and heart. Grounded on our mental development, there are three phase changes, each building on and expanding previous learning in our movement toward intelligent activity.

The concepts of **profundity** and **bifurcation** are introduced in terms of change. Profundity insinuates an intellectual complexity leading to great understanding, perceptiveness and knowledge. We believe that *the times in which we live and the opportunity to shape the future of humanity demand that each of us look within, recognizing and utilizing the amazing gifts of our human mind and heart to shape a new world.*

Bifurcation literally means to branch off into two separate parts. In terms of change, this alludes to a pending decision for each human, and perhaps humanity at large. We live in two worlds, one based on what we understand from Newtonian Physics and one based on what we don't understand but are able to speculate and feel about the Quantum Field. As change continues with every breath we take and every action we make, there is choice as to how we engage our role as co-creators of reality.

In the PBC books we explore very different ways to create change, each building on the former. There is no right or wrong—choice is a matter of the lessons we are learning and the growth we are seeking—yet it is clear that there is a split ahead where we will need to choose our way forward. One road continues the journey that has been punctuated by physical dominance, bureaucracy, hard competition, economic and political control, a disregard for truth and a variety of power scenarios. A second road, historically less-traveled, recognizes the connections among all humans, embracing the value of individualism and diversity as a contribution to the collective whole and the opportunities offered through creative imagination. This is the road that recognizes the virtues of inclusiveness and truth and the power of love and beauty, and moves us along the flow representing Quantum entanglement.

The PBC books are quite large, academically grounded and taking a consilience approach to large entangled issues emerging throughout the life experience. They wrote themselves. In the 1984 movie *Amadeus*, when a complaint is lodged against his work saying there are just too many notes, Mozart responds that there are just exactly as many notes as are needed. In the PBC books, there are exactly as many chapters as are needed, no more, no less. Yet, we realize that this rather massive amount of material is difficult to move through, and can prove overwhelming when coupled with the increasing demands of everyday life. This is why the little books that are part of the *Possibilities that are YOU!* emerged.

These ideas are meant for all of us! The Conscious Look Books are written for the *graduate student of life experience*. They are conversational in nature while retaining the depth of concepts, and specifically focused on sharing key concepts and looking at what those concepts mean to YOU. There are 22 little books available in paperback format from Amazon.com

This little book, which is excerpted from the larger PBC books, lays the foundation for this journey, and provides context in terms of the relationship of moral development, faith development and consciousness expansion. Section 7 in this book talks about how the PBC books and these little books relate. Further, we have included the readiness assessment instrument offered in the larger PBC books in the last section of this book in hopes that this will excite your imagination to vision the possible future.

We invite your thoughts and questions, not guaranteeing answers because there is still so much to learn, but happy to join in the conversation. Visit Mountain Quest Inn and Retreat Center www.mountainquestinn.com located in the Allegheny Mountains of West Virginia or email alex@mountainquestinstitute.com

Our gratitude to all those who take this journey with us, and a special thanks to the colleagues, partners, friends, family and visitors who touch our hearts and Mountain Quest in so many ways.

With Love and Light,

Alex, David, Arthur, Theresa and John

Contents

Introduction (Page 1)

Introduction

The Intelligent Social Change Journey (ISCJ) is a developmental journey of the body, mind and heart, moving from the heaviness of cause-and-effect linear extrapolations, to the fluidity of co-evolving with our environment, to the lightness of breathing our thought and feelings into reality. Grounded in development of our mental faculties, these are phase changes, each building on and expanding previous learning in our movement toward intelligent activity.

We are on this journey together. This is very much a *social* journey. Change does not occur in isolation. The deeper our understanding in relationship to others, the easier it is to move into the future. The quality of sympathy is needed as we navigate the linear, cause-and-effect characteristics of Phase 1 of this three-phase journey. The quality of empathy is needed to navigate the co-evolving liquidity of Phase 2. The quality of compassion is needed to navigate the connected breath of the Phase 3 creative leap. See the figure on the next page.

In the progression of learning to navigate change represented by the three phases of the ISCJ, we empower our selves, individuating and expanding. In the process, we become immersed in the human experience, a neuronal dance with the Universe, with

each of us in the driver's seat selecting our partners
and directing our dance steps.

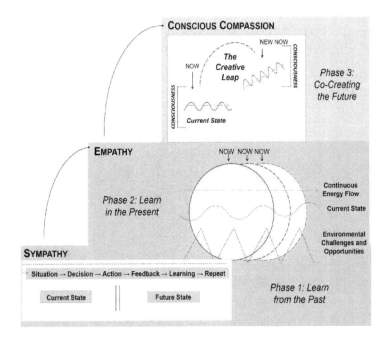

Figure 1. *The ISCJ Baseline Model. Each of the three
phases, including a larger visual of each, will be
introduced and detailed as we move through this little
book.*

Three critical movements during our journey,
consistent with movement through the phases, are
reflected in expanded consciousness, reduction of
forces and increased intelligent activity.

Consciousness is considered a state of awareness and a private, selective and continuous change process, a sequential set of ideas, thoughts, images, feelings and perceptions, and an understanding of the connections and relationships among them and our self. *Forces* occur when one type of energy affects another type of energy in a way such that they are moving in different directions, pressing against each other. Bounded (inward focused) and/or limited knowledge creates forces. There is a *Possibilities that are YOU!* volume on *Engaging Forces.* *Intelligent activity* represents a state of interaction where intent, purpose, direction, values and expected outcomes are clearly understood and communicated among all parties, reflecting wisdom and achieving a higher truth.

<<<<<<<<>>>>>>>

INSIGHT: **The ISCJ is a journey toward intelligent activity, which is a state of interaction where intent, purpose, direction, values and expected outcomes are clearly understood and communicated among all parties, reflecting wisdom and achieving a higher truth.**

<<<<<<<<>>>>>>>

Time and space play a significant role in the phase changes. Using Jung's psychological type classifications, feelings come from the past, sensations occur in the present, intuition is oriented to the future, and thinking embraces the past, present *and* future. Forecasting and visioning work is done at a point of change[2] when a balance is struck continuously between short-term and long-term survival. Salk describes this as a shift from Epoch A, dominated by ego and short-term considerations, to Epoch B, *where both being and ego co-exist.*[3] In the ISCJ, this shift occurs somewhere in Phase 2, with beingness advancing as we journey toward Phase 3.

<<<<<<<<>>>>>>>>
INSIGHT: **As Jung reminds us, feelings come from the past, sensations occur in the present, intuition is oriented to the future, and thinking embraces the past, present *and* future.**
<<<<<<<<>>>>>>>>

Let's explore the Intelligent Social Change Journey a bit deeper.

[Your Thoughts]

Phase 1: Learning from the Past

In Phase 1 of the Journey, *Learning from the Past*, we act on the physical and the physical changes; we "see" the changes with our sense of form, and therefore they are real. Causes have effects. Actions have consequences, both directly and indirectly, and sometimes delayed. Phase 1 reinforces the characteristics of how we interact with the simplest aspects of our world. The elements are predictable and repeatable and make us feel comfortable because we know what to expect and how to prepare for them. While these parts of the world do exist, our brain tends to automate the thinking around them and we do them with little conscious effort. The challenge with this is that they only remain predictable if all the causing influences remain constant ... and that just doesn't happen in the world of today!

The linear cause-and-effect phase of the ISCJ (Phase 1) calls for sympathy. Supporting and caring for the people involved in the change helps to mitigate the force of resistance, improving the opportunity for successful outcomes.

Characteristics, which are words or short phrases representing ideas developed in this phase, include linear and sequential, repeatability, engaging past learning, starting from current state, and cause and effect relationships.

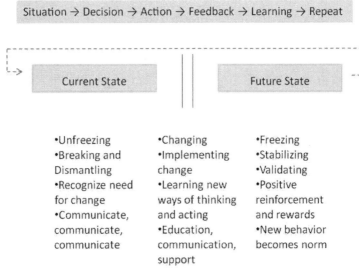

Situation → Decision → Action → Feedback → Learning → Repeat

Current State | Future State

•Unfreezing
•Breaking and Dismantling
•Recognize need for change
•Communicate, communicate, communicate

•Changing
•Implementing change
•Learning new ways of thinking and acting
•Education, communication, support

•Freezing
•Stabilizing
•Validating
•Positive reinforcement and rewards
•New behavior becomes norm

Figure 2. *Phase 1 of the ISCJ.*

In this phase, the nature of knowledge is characterized as a product of the past and, remember, knowledge is context sensitive and situation dependent, and is always partial and incomplete. Reflection during this phase of change is on reviewing the interactions and feedback, and determining cause-and-effect relationships. There is an inward focus, and a questioning of decisions and actions as reflected in the questions: What did I intend? What really happened? Why were there differences? What would I do the same? What would I do differently?

The cognitive shifts that are underway during this phase include: (1) recognition of the importance of feedback; (2) the ability to recognize systems and the impact of external forces; (3) recognition and location of "me" in the larger picture (building conscious awareness); and (4) pattern recognition and concept development. There is a *Possibilities that are YOU!* volume on *Connections as Patterns.* These reflections are critical to enabling the phase change to co-evolving (moving from Phase 1 to Phase 2).

Nature of Knowledge	Points of Reflection	Cognitive Shifts
• A product of the past • Knowledge is context sensitive and situation dependent • Knowledge is partial and incomplete	• Reviewing the interactions and feedback • Determining cause-and-effect relationships; logic • Inward focus • Questioning of decisions and actions: What did I intend? What really happened? Why were there differences? What would I do the same? What would I do differently	• Recognition of the importance of feedback • Ability to recognize systems and the impact of external forces • Recognition and location of "me" in the larger picture (building conscious awareness) • Beginning pattern recognition and early concept development

Table 1. *Characteristics of Phase 1 of the ISCJ: Linear and sequential; repeatable; engaging past learning; starting from current state; cause-and-effect relationships.*

[Your Thoughts]

Phase 2: Learning in the Present

As we expand toward Phase 2 of the ISCJ, we begin to recognize patterns; they emerge from experiences that repeat over and over. Recognition of patterns enables us to "see" (in our mind's eye) the relationship of events in terms of time and space, moving us out of an action and reaction mode into a position of co-evolving with our environment, and enabling us to better navigate a world full of diverse challenges and opportunities. It is at this stage that we move from understanding based on past cause-and-effect reactions to how things come together, to produce new things both in the moment at hand and at a future point in time.

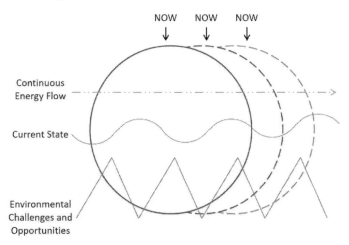

Figure 3. *Phase 2 of the ISCJ.*

There is a *Possibilities that are YOU!* volume on *Staying on the Path*. This little book describes ideas that emerge along the path of life, ideas that begin the conceptual and developmental expansion necessary for spontaneous change.

Learning in the Present (Phase 2) takes us to the next level of thinking and feeling about how we interact with our world, including the interesting area of human social interactions. In Phase 2 patterns grow into concepts, higher mental thought, and we begin the search for a higher level of truth. Although complex, the somewhat recognizable patterns enable us to explore and progress through uncertainty and the unknown, making life more interesting and enjoyable. Sustainability in the co-evolving state of Phase 2 requires empathy, which provides a direct understanding of another individual, and a heightened awareness of the context of their lives and their desires and needs in the moment at hand. While not yet achieving the creative leap of the intuitional (represented in Phase 3), we are clearly developing higher mental faculties and instinctive knowledge of the workings of the Universe, which helps cultivate intuition and develop insights in service to our self and society.

Characteristics, which are words or short phrases representing ideas developed in this phase, include recognition of patterns; social interaction; and co-evolving with the environment through continuous learning, quick response, robustness, flexibility, adaptability and alignment.

<<<<<<<<>>>>>>>

INSIGHT: **Empathy provides a direct understanding of another individual, and a heightened awareness of the context of their lives and their desires and needs in the moment at hand.**

<<<<<<<<>>>>>>>

The nature of knowledge is characterized in terms of expanded cooperation and collaboration, and knowledge sharing and social learning. There is also the conscious *questioning of why*, and the *pursuit of truth*. Reflection includes a deepening of conceptual thinking and, through cooperation and collaboration, the ability to connect the power of diversity and individuation to the larger whole. There is an increasing outward focus, with the recognition of different world views and the exploration of information from different perspectives, and expanded knowledge capacities.

<<<<<<<<>>>>>>>

INSIGHT: **In Phase 2 there is the conscious questioning of why, and the continuing pursuit of truth.**

<<<<<<<<>>>>>>>

Cognitive shifts that are underway include: (1) the ability to recognize and apply patterns at all levels within a domain of knowledge to predict outcomes; (2) a growing understanding of complexity; (3) increased connectedness of choices, recognition of direction you are heading, and expanded meaning-making; and (4) an expanded ability to bisociate ideas resulting in increased creativity. There is a *Possibilities that are YOU!* volume on *ME as Co-Creator.*

Nature of Knowledge	Points of Reflection	Cognitive Shifts
• Expanded knowledge sharing and social learning • Engaging cooperation and collaboration • Questioning of why? • Pursuit of truth	• Deeper development of conceptual thinking (higher mental thought) • Through cooperation and collaboration ability to connect the power of diversity and individuation to the larger whole • Outward focus • Recognition of different world views and exploration of information from different perspectives • Expanded knowledge capacities	• The ability to recognize and apply patterns at all levels within a domain of knowledge to predict outcomes • A growing understanding of complexity • Increased connectedness of choices • Recognition of direction you are heading • Expanded meaning-making • Expanded ability to bisociate ideas resulting in increased creativity

Table 2. *Characteristics of Phase 2 of the ISCJ: Co-Evolving (requires empathy). Recognition of patterns; Co-evolving with environment through continuous learning, quick response, robustness, flexibility, adaptability, alignment.*

Phase 3: Co-Creating the Future

The creative leap of Phase 3, *Co-Creating the Future*, requires the ability to tap into the larger intuitional field that energetically connects all people. This can only be accomplished when energy is focused outward in service to the larger whole, requiring a deeper connection to others. Compassion deepens that connection. Thus, each phase of the Intelligent Social Change Journey calls for an increasing depth of connection to others, moving from sympathy to empathy to compassion.

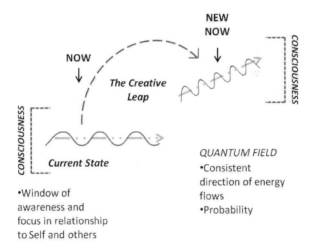

Figure 4. *Phase 3 of the ISCJ.*

Phase characteristics, which are words or short phrases representing ideas developed in this phase, include creative imagination; recognition of global Oneness; mental in service to the intuitive; balancing senses; bringing together time (the past, present and future); knowing; beauty; and wisdom.

The nature of knowledge is characterized as a recognition that with knowledge comes responsibility. There is a conscious pursuit of larger truth, and knowledge is selectively used as a measure of effectiveness.

Reflection includes the valuing of creative ideas, asking the larger questions: How does this idea serve humanity? Are there any negative consequences? There is an openness to other's ideas, a questioning with humility: What if this idea is right? Are my beliefs or other mental models limiting my thoughts? Are hidden assumptions or feelings interfering with intelligent activity?

<<<<<<<<>>>>>>>

INSIGHT: **There is a conscious pursuit of larger truth, an openness to other's ideas, and a questioning with humility.**

<<<<<<<<>>>>>>>

Cognitive shifts that are underway include: (1) a sense and knowing of Oneness; (2) development of both the lower (logic) and upper (conceptual) mental faculties, which work in concert with the emotional guidance system; (3) recognition of self as a co-creator of reality; (4) the ability to engage in intelligent activity; and (5) a developing ability to tap into the intuitional plane at will.

Nature of Knowledge	Points of Reflection	Cognitive Shifts
• Recognition that with knowledge comes responsibility • Conscious pursuit of larger truth • Knowledge selectively used as a measure of effectiveness	• Valuing of creative ideas • Asking the larger questions: How does this idea serve humanity? Are there any negative consequences? • Openness to other's ideas • Questioning with humility: What if this idea is right? Are my beliefs or other mental models limiting my thought? Are hidden assumptions or feelings interfering with intelligent activity?	• A sense and knowing of Oneness • Development of both the lower (logic) and upper (conceptual) mental faculties, which work in concert with the emotional guidance system • Applies patterns across domains of knowledge for greater good (wisdom) • Recognition of self as a co-creator of reality • The ability to engage in intelligent activity • Developing the ability to tap into the intuitional plane at will

Table 3. *Characteristics of Phase 3 of the ISCJ: Creative Leap (requires compassion). Creative imagination; recognition of global Oneness; mental in service to the intuitive; balancing senses; brining together past, present and future; knowing; beauty; wisdom.*

There are *Possibilities that are YOU!* volumes on many of the core areas touched in describing Phase 3 of the ISCJ. These include: *All Things in Balance*, *Knowing*, *Transcendent Beauty*, *Truth in Context*, *Seeking Wisdom*, and *The Creative Leap*. The full listing of all 22 Conscious Look Books is included on Page 81 in this book.

[Your Thoughts]

4. Cognitive-Based Ordering of Change

As a cognitive-based ordering of change, we forward the concept of logical levels of learning consistent with levels of change developed by anthropologist Gregory Bateson, which is based on the work in logic and mathematics of Bertrand Russell. This logical typing was both a mathematical theory and a law of nature, recognizing long before neuroscience research findings confirmed the relationship of the mind/brain, which show that we literally create our reality, with thought affecting the physical structure of the brain and the physical structure of the brain affecting thought. There is a *Possibilities that are YOU!* volume on *ME as Co-Creator.*

Bateson's levels of change range from simplistic habit formation (which he calls Learning I) to large-scale change in the evolutionary process of the human (which he calls Learning IV), with each higher level synthesizing and organizing the levels below it, and thus creating a greater impact on people and organizations.[4] This is a hierarchy of logical levels, ordered groupings within a system, with the implication that as the levels reach toward the source or beginning **there is a sacredness of power or importance informing this hierarchy of**

values.[5] This structure is consistent with the phase changes of the Intelligent Social Change Journey.

INSIGHT: **Similar to Bateson's levels of change, each higher phase of the Intelligent Social Change Journey synthesizes and organizes the levels below it, thus creating a greater impact in interacting with the world.**

<<<<<<<◇>>>>>>>

With *Learning 0* representing the status quo, a particular behavioral response to a specific situation, *Learning I* (first-order change) is stimulus-response conditioning (cause-and-effect change), which includes learning simple skills such as walking, eating, and driving. These basic skills are pattern forming, becoming habits, which occur through repetitiveness without conceptualizing the content. For example, we don't have to understand concepts of motion and movement in order to learn to walk. Animals engage in Learning I. Because it is not necessary to understand the concepts, or underlying theories, no questions of reality are raised. Learning I occurs in Phase 1 of the ISCJ.

Learning II (second-order change) is deuteron learning and includes creation, or a change of context inclusive of new images or concepts, or shifts the understanding of, and connections among, existing concepts such that meaning may be interpreted. These changes are based on mental constructs that *depend on a sense of reality*.[6] While these concepts may represent real things, relations or qualities, they also may be symbolic, specifically created for the situation at hand. They provide the means for reconstructing existing concepts, using one reality to modify another, from which new ways of thinking and behaviors emerge. Argyris and Schon's concept of double loop learning reflects Level II change.[7] Learning II occurs in Phase 2.

Learning III (third-order change) requires thinking beyond our current logic, calling us to change our system of beliefs and values, and offering different sets of alternatives from which choices can be made. Suggesting that Learning III is learning about the concepts used in Learning II, Bateson says, "In transcending the promises and habits of Learning II, one will gain 'a freedom from its bondages,' bondages we characterize, for example, as 'drive,' 'dependency,' 'pride,' and 'fatalism.' One might learn to change the premises acquired by Learning II and to readily choose among the roles through which we express concepts and thus the 'self.'[8]

<<<<<<<◇>>>>>>

INSIGHT: **There is a freedom that occurs as we leave behind the thinking patterns of Phase 2 and open to the choices and discoveries of Phase 3.**

<<<<<<<◇>>>>>>

Similarly, Berman defines Learning III as, "an experience in which a person suddenly realizes the arbitrary nature of his or her own paradigm."[9] This is the breaking open of our personal mental models, our current logic, losing the differential of subject/object, blending into connection while simultaneously following pathways of diverse belief systems. Learning III occurs as we move into Phase 3 of the ISCJ.

Learning IV deals with revolutionary change, getting outside the system to look at the larger system of systems, awakening to something completely new, different, unique and transformative. This is the space of *incluessence* introduced in the Preface, a future state far beyond that which we know to dream. As Bateson described this highest level of change: "The individual mind is immanent but not only in the body. It is immanent in pathways and messages outside the body; and there is a larger Mind of which the individual mind is only a sub-system. This larger Mind is comparable to God and is perhaps what people mean by 'God,' but it is still immanent in the total interconnected social system and planetary ecology."[10]

Table 4 below is a comparison of the Phases of the ISCJ and the four Levels of Learning espoused by Bateson based on the work in logic and mathematics of Bertrand Russell, and, as detailed above, supported by Argyris and Schon, Berman, and McWhinney.

Phase of the Intelligent Social Change Journey	Level of Learning [NOTE: LEARNING 0 represents the status quo; a behavioral response to a specific situation.]
PHASE 1: Cause and Effect (Requires sympathy) • Linear, and Sequential • Repeatable • Engaging past learning • Starting from current state • Cause and effect relationships	**LEARNING 1: (First order change)** • Stimulus-response conditioning • Includes learning simple skills such as walking, eating and driving • Basic skills are pattern forming, becoming habits occurring through repetitiveness without conceptualizing the content • No questions of reality
PHASE 2: Co-Evolving (Requires empathy) • Recognition of patterns • Social interaction • Co-evolving with environment through continuous learning, quick response, robustness, flexibility, adaptability, alignment.	**LEARNING II: (Deutero Learning)** (Second order change) • Includes creation or change of context inclusive of new images or concepts • Shifts the understanding of, and connections among, existing concepts such that meaning may be interpreted • Based on mental constructions that depend on a sense of reality
[Moving into Phase 3] **PHASE 3: Creative Leap** (Requires compassion) • Creative imagination • Recognition of global Oneness • Mental in service to the intuitive • Balancing senses • Bringing together past, present and future • Knowing; Beauty; Wisdom	**LEARNING III: (Third order change)** • Thinking beyond current logic • Changing our system of beliefs and values • Different sets of alternatives from which choices can be made • Freedom from bondages **LEARNING IV:** • Revolutionary change • Getting outside the system to look at the larger system of systems • Awakening to something completely new, different, unique and transformative • Tapping into the larger Mind of which the individual mind is a sub-system

Table 4. *Comparison of phases of the ISCJ with Levels of Learning.*

An example of Learning IV is Budda's use of intuitional thought to understand others. He used his ability to think in greater and greater ways to help people cooperate and share together, and think better. Learning IV is descriptive of controlled intuition in support of the creative leap in Phase 3 of the ISCJ, perhaps moving beyond what we can comprehend at this point in time, perhaps deepening the connections of sympathy, empathy and compassion to unconditional love.

[Your Thoughts]

5. The related journey of faith and moral development, and consciousness.

Belief and faith provide inner strength, and play a very large role in our personal development. We have a belief—about ourselves and our place in the world—and have faith that our belief is true. This is similar to how our ancient philosophers defined knowledge as "justified true belief," a belief that has been proven true by acting on it and seeing the results.

<<<<<<<◇>>>>>>>

INSIGHT: **Belief and faith provide inner strength, and play a very large role in our personal development.**

<<<<<<<◇>>>>>>>

A belief is *a feeling* that something is good, right or valuable. It is a feeling of trust in the worth or ability of someone or something, and might even be considered *a state or habit of mind* in which trust or confidence is placed in some person or thing. Belief is also related to a conviction of the truth. Note that a conviction is both a feeling and a state or habit of mind.

Think about the beliefs you have. Beliefs change how we perceive the world, and then our biology—

the way we think and act—adapts to those beliefs. We each have a unique autobiography that includes different beliefs and personal goals. As David Bennet always says: *What we believe leads to what we think leads to our knowledge base, which leads to our actions.* For example, if we believe that we cannot do something, our thoughts, feelings, and actions will be such that, at best, that objective will be much more difficult to accomplish! If we believe we *can* accomplish something, we are much more likely to do so ... and this results from choice, not genes.

<<<<<<<◇>>>>>>>

INSIGHT: **What we believe leads to what we think leads to our knowledge base, which leads to our actions.**

<<<<<<<◇>>>>>>>

This description presents a chain of logic that ties our beliefs to our actions and our successes—or failures. Our beliefs heavily influence our mindset or frame of reference, the direction from which we perceive, reflect, and comprehend an external experience or situation. Thus, beliefs influence how we interpret and feel about the information that comes into our senses, what insights we develop, what ideas we create and what parts of the incoming information are most important to us.

Through observation, reflection and conceptualization we create our understanding and meaning of the external world. How we see the external world and how we emotionally feel about external events drive our actions and reactions. And how we act and react to our external environment influences whether we are successful or not, that is, whether we achieve our goals or not.

To understand the connection between beliefs, which are patterns in the mind, and the physiology of the brain, consider the following story. You have just received a phone call from the local police telling you that your son has been killed in an automobile accident. Now, envision your feelings, emotions, and behavior, the changes in your body, your actions, and so on. These are all real physical responses which can be observed and measured. Two minutes later you receive a second call from the same policeman who tells you that there was a mistake and it was not your son who was killed. Now, imagine the changes in your body responses, thoughts and feelings. All that happened during those two minutes was created by you, caused by your perception of an event that had occurred. Only nothing really happened. Your son was perfectly healthy the entire time. All of the changes were created by the beliefs, thoughts and feelings within your own mind.

As you can see, beliefs and biology are not independent; they are intimately connected through the relationship of patterns of the mind and the physiology of the brain. And patterns of neuronal firings and changing synaptic strengths can, and do, create and release hormones that change the body … very much based on thoughts and feelings.

Thus, *positive and negative beliefs affect every aspect of life*. This is a finding that has widespread application. When we recognize how powerful our beliefs are—recognizing that they are core pivot points in the hierarchy of life—we hold the key to freedom and **we can change our minds**. We can experience, interpret, and anticipate our responses to external events, and *decide* on our response *as we choose*. Our thoughts can change our brains; our brains affect our thoughts and can change our body.

Today we have the benefit of neuroscience research to figure all this out. But, way back early last century, Henry Ford, the car giant, had it right, and he didn't know what we know! While Henry is remembered for introducing the efficiency of the assembly line, he also said that if you think you're right or you think you're wrong, you're right. *He* was right.

<<<<<<<◇>>>>>>>

INSIGHT: **Positive and negative beliefs affect every aspect of our lives. "If you think you're right or if you think you're wrong, you're right!**

<<<<<<<◇>>>>>>>

Many of the same words used to define *beliefs* are used to define *faith*, that is, faith can be considered *a strong belief or trust* in someone or something, or *accepting something without question*. Of course, faith can also be a specific reference to belief in the existence of God or refer to other strong religious feelings or beliefs. In this context, faith is a *living attribute* which reflects a religious experience that is both genuine and personal.

The term faith may also carry with it the idea of obligation from loyalty, and thus is connected to trust. From those who dig deeply into meanings of words, faith is independent of reason, with reason and faith two separate approaches, and faith having a higher truth value. In other words, there are some questions that reason cannot address, some larger truths that can only be achieved through faith.

As we reflect on this journey of life and the changes that come with experience and maturity, it is amazing to realize that the journey of faith, the journey of moral development and the journey of expanded consciousness *are part of the same journey!*

<<<<<<<◇>>>>>>>

INSIGHT: **The journey of faith, moral development and expanded consciousness are part of the same journey!**

<<<<<<<◇>>>>>>>

Let's explore this relationship through the eyes of three well-known and highly respected researchers: the theologian James W. Fowler,[11] the psychologist Lawrence Kohlberg,[12] and the psychiatrist David R. Hawkins.[13] This exploration is important, because whatever age you happen to be right now, as long as you continue living, you will grow older every day and, frankly, these things become VERY important as you move closer to the end of this life. We're always asking ourselves: Have I learned enough? Have I done enough? How can I make a bigger difference? And, since life is finite, whatever we decide still needs doing, we'd better do now!

As a baseline, and by way of review, the ISCJ focuses on three phase changes, with each phase building on/expanding from the previous phase. The first phase of our learning journey is based on understanding past cause-and-effect relationships through the lower mental thinking of logic. When we begin to recognize patterns, we move into higher mental conceptual thinking, and begin to co-evolve with our environment, taking patterns from the past and, in the "now," using those patterns to make decisions about the future. This co-evolving requires a deeper understanding of self (thoughts and emotions) and developing an empathy for others with whom we are co-evolving.

As we develop a higher understanding of patterns and connections, we begin to recognize that everything is connected and we are all part of a larger ecosystem, whether we call that the consciousness field, the Quantum field or the God field. With this understanding, compassion for others blooms. This phase of our developmental journey introduces the creative leap, as we now recognize the power of our thoughts and feelings, and fully take on our role as co-creators of our reality.

<<<<<<<◇>>>>>>>

INSIGHT: **As we develop a higher understanding of patterns and connections, we begin to recognize that everything is connected and we are all part of a larger ecosystem.**

<<<<<<<◇>>>>>>>

Now, back to our three researchers.

First, delving into the psychology of human development and the search for meaning, the theologian Fowler proposed *six stages of faith-development* which correlate to development of the self across the life-span. Note that this does not mean that every individual makes it through all these stages during a single lifetime!

Second, looking through the lens of moral development, the psychologist Kohlberg identified *a hierarchical relationship among six stages*, with each subsequent stage reorganizing and integrating the preceding one, providing the basis for moral decisions. Thus, this sequence is fixed, although timing is different for different people.

Third, the psychiatrist Hawkins uses the concept of levels of consciousness to represent *calibrated levels correlated with a specific process of consciousness*, which includes emotions, perceptions, attitudes, worldviews and spiritual beliefs. He mapped the energy field of consciousness, with the levels ranging from 0 to 1,000.

Now, what are these stages all about and how do they link together? The first faith stage is *intuitive-projective*, when a young child uses speech and symbols to organize experiences into meaning units. This is a fantasy-filled, imitative phase, prior to development of mental capabilities.

Stage of faith development	Stage of moral development	Levels of Consciousness
STAGE ONE: *Intuitive-Projective* • Speech and symbolic representation to organize sensory experience into meaning units.		

Table 5: *Preparation for ISCJ Phase 1*

It is in the second faith stage of *mythic-literal* where the ten-year-old, capable of both inductive and deductive reasoning, constructs an orderly, linear and dependable world, primarily using story. In terms of moral development, we are in the first stage, where there are consequences to actions, with power of authority and punishment. This is part of **Phase 1 of the ISCJ**, and, in consciousness development, we are moving through the first 150 levels which include shame, guilt, apathy, grief, fear, desire and anger.

Stage of faith development	Stage of moral development	Levels of Consciousness
STAGE TWO: *Mythic-literal* • Inductive and deductive reasoning • Orderly, linear and dependable world	STAGE ONE: • Power of authority and punishment • Consequences of actions STAGE TWO: *Instrumental Exchange* • Conventional reasoning • Balancing self-interests with others	20-15: Moves through shame, Guilt, apathy, Grief, Fear, Desire and Anger (dependent on individual) 175: Pride

Table 6: *ISCJ Phase 1 (requires sympathy). Focus on: linear and sequential, repeatable, engaging past learning, starting from current state, cause-and-effect relationships.*

In the third faith stage, there is both a reflection on self and movement into a social, conformist stage. Similarly, the second stage of moral development moves through conventional reasoning to the beginnings of balancing self-interests with the interests of others, which, in stage three has an interpersonal relationship focus, seeking approval of significant others. In the consciousness expansion journey, at this level pride and courage are important.

Stage of faith development	Stage of moral development	Levels of Consciousness
STAGE THREE: *Synthetic-Conventional* • Reflection on self • Social, conformist stage STAGE FOUR: *Individuative-Reflective* • Developing system of meaning. • Executive ego; Critical thinking. • Incorporating others perspectives.	STAGE THREE: • Interpersonal relationships focus • Internalized rules meeting desires and for approval of significant others STAGE FOUR: *Doing one's duty.* • Internalized rules maintained for their own sake rather than for the sake of others.	200: Courage [Moving out of negativity] 250: Neutrality 310: Willingness

Table 7: *ON THE CUSP between ISCJ Phase 1 and Phase 2. Focus on interpersonal relationship, moving toward co-evolving and developing empathy.*

Phase 2 of the ISCJ focuses on co-evolving, with social interaction and the individuated human working together. In faith development, we are in the fourth stage, what is called *individuative-reflective*, where the individual develops a system of meaning while incorporating others perspectives. In the moral development journey, we are also in stage four, where rules have been internalized and are *obeyed for their own sake* rather than for the sake of others. At this stage, consciousness levels move through willingness and acceptance toward reason.

We are still in **Phase 2** but **moving toward Phase 3 of the ISCJ** as we enter the fifth stage of faith development, a way of seeing, knowing and committing beyond logic, which includes seeing both sides of an issue simultaneously and recognizing the interrelatedness of things.

<<<<<<<◇>>>>>>>

INSIGHT: **We are moving toward Phase 3 of the ISCJ when we develop a way of seeing, knowing and committing beyond logic.**

<<<<<<<◇>>>>>>>

We have also entered stage five of moral development, considering each situation differently, developing rules and principles for good decision-making and behavior, and *recognizing the need for flexibility and relativism* in rules of behavior and protection of all individuals. In other words, there is not one answer, but many answers, such that we must use our learned discernment to choose the best course of action! On our consciousness journey we have moved further into love, and an interest in spiritual awareness is emerging.

<<<<<<<◇>>>>>>>

INSIGHT: **As we move toward love in our consciousness journey, we enter stage five of both faith and moral development.**

<<<<<<<◇>>>>>>>

Stage of faith development	Stage of moral development	Levels of consciousness
STAGE FIVE: *Conjunctive* • Way of seeing, knowing and committing beyond logic. • Seeing both sides of an issue simultaneously. • Recognize interrelatedness of things • Ironic imagination.	STAGE FIVE: *Contractual Orientation* • Understand abstract moral principles. • Consider each situation differently. • Develop rules and principles for good decision-making and behavior. • Recognize need for flexibility and relativism in rules of behavior and protection of all individuals.	350: Acceptance 400: reason 500: Love [Interest in spiritual awareness]

Table 8: *ISCJ Phase 2: Co-Evolving (requires empathy). Individuated human; recognition of patterns; social interaction; co-evolving with environment through continuous learning, quick responses, robustness, flexibility, adaptability, alignment.*

As we are firmly in **Phase 3 of the ISCJ**, *the creative leap*, with recognition of global Oneness and the development of compassion, we have entered the sixth stage of faith development. This is a *transcendent actuality of unconditional love and universal compassion*. There is a selfless passion to serve others and a desire to transform the world. This is also the sixth stage of moral development, where the person has individuated while simultaneously taking actions based on *universal moral principles*. This individual is able to accurately take the perspective of each person and group affected. In our consciousness expansion journey, we now move into joy and peace, and *the good of mankind becomes a primary goal.*

Stage of faith development	Stage of moral development	Levels of consciousness
STAGE SIX: Universalizing Faith • Transcendent actuality • Unconditional love • Universalizing compassion • Selfless passion to serve others • Desire to transform the world	STAGE SIX: *Universal Ethical Principle Orientation* • Universalizable moral principles • Personal commitment • Conduct drive by own ideas • Informed moral imagination • Accurately take perspective of others	540: Joy 600: Peace [Good of mankind becomes primary goal] 700-1,000: Enlightenment

Table 9. *ISCJ Phase 3: Creative Leap (requires compassion). Creative imagination; recognition of global Oneness; mental in service to the intuitive; balancing senses; bringing together past, present and future; knowing; beauty; wisdom.*

<<<<<<<◇>>>>>>

INSIGHT: **Along with the transcendent actuality of unconditional love and compassion, we move into joy and peace, and the good of mankind becomes a primary goal.**

<<<<<<<◇>>>>>>

The close relationship of growth and expansion among moral development, faith development, consciousness expansion and the ISCJ is *not* a coincidence. The ISCJ is a developmental journey that encompasses all aspects of what it is to be human, and there is growth and expansion from *all* of those aspects.

As we have come to recognize over the past century, the human is holistic, that is, our physical, mental, emotional and spiritual natures work together to create a whole human. One part cannot be separated out from the others. Thus, faith development and moral development, along with consciousness expansion, are all interconnected with the Intelligent Social Change Journey.

[Your Thoughts]

6. The ISCJ is a return journey!

The phase changes of the ISCJ might feel familiar to the journeyer, because they are. As babies, we are born connected to our mothers and families and to the larger energies surrounding us. This is the place we begin breathing our thoughts and feelings into reality (in the ISCJ this is represented in Phase 3). Then, around 4th grade, when we begin the process of individuation, we look to those around us as models, living in the NOW and very much co-evolving with, flowing with, our environment (in the ISCJ this is represented as Phase 2).

By the mid-teens we are immersed in the learning of cause and effect, whether imposed by parents, schools, religion or society. There is a heaviness here; with rules to be learned, and consequences to actions taken outside those rule sets (in the ISCJ this is represented as Phase 1). As we move toward adulthood, **this is the starting point** of the Intelligent Social Change Journey, the focus of this little book. What we are acknowledging here is that *this is a return journey*! In our infancy and early childhood, if we *could* remember, we have moved from Phase 3 to Phase 2 to Phase 1, where we start the *conscious journey of expansion* in Phase 1. See Figure 5.

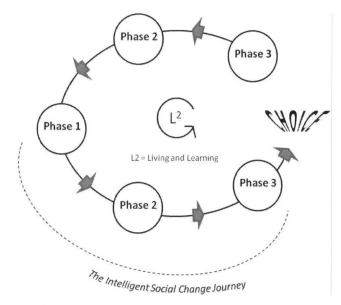

Figure 5. *The human journey of choice.*

In Phase 1, within the framework of our local environment and with a focus on the geosphere (the physical), diversity thrives on freedom as we follow our passions and individuate as we are able, deciding what we like and what we don't like. While there is much to learn in this phase, today as a global world, the large majority of our youth move rapidly into the NOW and co-evolving of Phase 2.

In Phase 2, with a focus on the biosphere (living organisms), these young minds are not tethered by action and reaction; they understand *concepts*, higher mental thinking, the way things are connected and the relationships among those connections. Through their interactions with others around the world, they honor diversity and have developed an empathetic understanding of other cultures. People are people, each unique and creative, each with likes and dislikes, each with passions, and each choosing where to focus their energy and their creative juices.

INSIGHT: **Virtue grows from diversity as we recognize the interconnectivity and interdependence of humanity, and move toward an understanding of Oneness and the thoughts and actions that Oneness advances**.

And this is the entry into the expansion that occurs in Phase 3 of the ISCJ. The creative leap of this phase requires the ability to tap into the larger intuitional field that energetically connects all people. This can only be accomplished when energy is focused outward in service to the larger whole, requiring a deeper connection to others. Compassion deepens that connection. As can be seen and has been introduced earlier in this book, each phase of the ISCJ calls for an increasing depth of connection to others, moving from sympathy to empathy to compassion. *Conscious Compassion* is a volume of *Possibilities that are YOU!*

Virtue grows from this Journey-nurtured diversity as we recognize the interconnectivity and interdependence of humanity, and strengthen our connections to the *Noosphere* ("a human sphere, a sphere of reflection, of conscious invention, of conscious souls").[14] At this point in our journey, we move toward an understanding of Oneness and the thoughts and actions that Oneness advances. For example, balance and beauty are choices that expand humanity beyond the limits of virtue to a larger frame of reference, helping us move fully into co-creating our collective reality. There are *Possibilities that are YOU!* volumes on *Living Virtues for Today*, *Transcendent Beauty* and *All Things in Balance.*

7. The Bifurcation: The Choice[15]

A Self Readiness Assessment to prepare for the profound choice facing humankind today.[16]

Every life is a journey, and at every point in this journey we are in the process of becoming something else. So it is difficult to secure a robust foundation from which we take our next steps. There can be *vastly different perspectives on where we are at any point in time*. What is known to one is unknown to others, or perceived very differently. What seems real to one person can be totally unreal to another. *Your truth* is considered just a perception by others, and vice versa. For example, one person's terrorist is another person's war hero, an unfortunate reality that we collectively face in challenging times.

Differences in perception of reality, belief and truth often cause conflict between those who differ. Historically, these differences have caused arguments, ill feelings and even wars. However, if we can get past considering differences as barriers, and tune our mindset to *view differences as potential for creative living and innovation*, we can expand and accelerate what we individually and collectively are capable of achieving. By engaging others in this mindset, we can also *amplify the value* of what we achieve by helping those around us achieve more as well.

There is stability only in the dynamic process of change, that is, the knowing that change is a dynamic process of life. There is within the human a continuous need for more and different, an underlying desire to experience, and through this experiencing the shifting and changing of desires opening an ever-expanding frontier of choice. We *need* change. We *crave* change. We cannot go backwards. Change is a journey into the future, a global future requiring recognition of an entangled humanity, considering the impact of our decisions and actions on others and our environment.

<<<<<<◇>>>>>>

INSIGHT: **There is stability only in the dynamic process of change, that is, the knowing that change is a dynamic process of life.**

<<<<<<◇>>>>>>

Understanding and assessing readiness for change is a vital component of change leadership. Since new knowledge is developed based on our existing knowledge base through the associative patterning process,[17] it is important to relate new thought to previously developed, and accepted, thought. Yet, at this particular point in the history of humanity—in the midst of a conscious expansion of our human capacity and understanding—the *rules* are changing; indeed, *we* are beginning to recognize higher patterns and truths that heretofore have been unrecognizable, far beyond the upper thresholds of all but a few advanced humans such as an Einstein, Leonardo Da Vinci, Pope John Paul II, the 14th Dalai Lama, Mother Teresa, Bill Gates, Thomas Edison, Eleanor Roosevelt, Mozart, Nelson Mandela, Martin Luther King, Desmond Tutu and others of whom you are aware who have touched us in service to create a better world.

<<<<<<<◇>>>>>>

INSIGHT: **At this particular point in the history of humanity, the rules are changing. We are beginning to recognize higher patterns and truths that heretofore have been unrecognizable.**

<<<<<<<◇>>>>>>

Are we ready?

As we move away from predictable patterns susceptible to logic, we are increasingly reliant on our "gut" instinct, an internal sense of knowing that can tap into the intuitional plane. Yet, this knowing can only serve us if we "know" what to do with it, how to act. *Development of our mental faculties is essential to acting.* To prepare ourselves to understand current situational assessments and potential future opportunities and threats, it is essential that we learn to **identify, understand, interpret, make decisions, and take appropriate**

action to counter new threats and recognize and embrace new opportunities utilizing this sense of *knowing*, which is, to some extent, available to each human.

Remember, we are on a developmental journey of the body, mind and heart—what we call the Intelligent Social Change Journey—moving from the heaviness of cause-and-effect linear extrapolations, to the fluidity of co-evolving with our environment, to the lightness of breathing our thought and feelings into reality. Grounded in development of our mental faculties, these are phase changes, each building on and expanding previous learning in our movement toward *intelligent activity*.[18]

Priming the Pump

To create the world that we desire, a major learning of individuals leading change is the need to measure for the future while learning from the past. To do this we vision the future as if it is here today, and perceive the processes and outcomes that are occurring from that frame of reference.

Similarly, thought patterns and behaviors in this future environment will be different than those we experience in today's world. Thus, the 55 statements that follow in this self readiness assessment instrument represent looking at change from the viewpoint of the future, reflecting the ability to use all three phases of the Intelligent Social Change Journey model: the cause and effect, linear logic of

Phase 1; the co-evolving, co-creating based on conceptual thought and the search for truth of Phase 2; and the balancing of senses, tapping into the intuitional and creative leap of Phase 3. This is a first step to laying aside our mental models and fully engaging a holistic approach to change. Since there are so many concepts—and their application—connected to the full and successful use of these phases, this instrument serves as an initial exposure, an overview (or for some a review) of important concepts developed throughout the book: *The Profundity and Bifurcation of Change.*

All statements and the concepts they represent are not equal, and may or may not apply at any given time to the stage or extent of desired change. For example, an individual or organization may be ready for the creative leap in one domain of knowledge or situation, and lacking in another area where the mental preparation in terms of recognition of patterns, conceptual thinking and developing an understanding of truth has not yet been achieved. However, all of these concepts—and more as we continue learning about ourselves, others, and the Universe in which we live—will eventually emerge in the journey of change.

The Statements

We have chosen to use a simple, comfortable five-point Likert scale,[19] which allows for a neutral response (3) so that the responder can, whether in the conscious or unconscious, just sit with an idea for a period of time. All of these concepts emerge as you move through the Intelligent Social Change Journey, each unfolding on the other. These concepts are also included in depth in the five Parts of *The Profundity and Bifurcation of Change* and many of them appear throughout the 22 volumes of the *Possibilities that are YOU!* series (see page 81). It is hoped that these 55 core statements will stimulate your thought about the possible future.

There one five-point Likert scale for you to use with each statement. Your response would be one of the following:

(1) Strongly Disagree → (2) Disagree → (3) Neutral → (4) Agree → (5) Strongly Agree

As you respond, please take into account your *cognitive availability*, that is, how closed or open you are to the ideas presented in the statement. Also, take into account your feelings, that is, how *comfortable* are you with the concept.

Note that your responses indicate the truth of each statement to you personally. After you have made your choices (usually your first response is the best one), think about or write down the rationale for your choice. This will help you understand why you think/feel the way you do.

The brief paragraph below each statement will provide a surface level of understanding regarding the concept, and will point to the Chapter/Part of the larger book, *The Profundity and Bifurcation of Change*, and/or the volume of the *Possibilities that are YOU!* series, where additional information can be found. The intent of these short paragraphs is to stimulate and titillate. There are no right or wrong responses; each person is quite different. However, you are planting new ideas into your subconscious as you move through this exercise, and that may just trigger a past thought or experience that makes sense. Above all, please have fun as you navigate these potentially new, yet somehow familiar, ideas!

PART I: Laying the Groundwork

1. The interpretation and meaning of incoming information is very much a function of pre-existing patterns in the brain.

Characteristics: Incoming information is associated with related patterns you have in your mind, experiences and the patterns associated with those experiences. The new pattern focused on the situation at hand is built on these associations, that is, relationships with other patterns already in your mind that provide meaning. [See Chapter 1/Part I; PY16.]

Choose: (1) Strongly Disagree → (2) Disagree → (3) Neutral → (4) Agree → (5) Strongly Agree

Provide rationale/supporting evidence:

2. I recognize that my knowledge is incomplete and imperfect, and choose to be a continuous learner.

Characteristics: Knowledge is context sensitive and situation dependent. Any small shift in the context or situation may require shifting or expanding knowledge, which in turn drives different decisions and actions to achieve the desired outcome(s). Further, no single person can know all there is to know regarding a specific subject. Thus, interacting with others who have expertise in a domain of knowledge and continuously learning from each other provides the best opportunity for making wise decisions. [See Chapter 2/Part I; PY15 and throughout series.]

Choose: (1) Strongly Disagree → (2) Disagree → (3) Neutral → (4) Agree → (5) Strongly Agree

Provide rationale/supporting evidence:

3. In most situations I move toward intelligent activity.

Characteristics: Intelligent activity is a state of interaction where intent, purpose, direction, values and expected outcomes are clearly understood and communicated among all parties, reflecting wisdom and achieving a higher truth. When knowledge is connected to other knowledge, shared and expanded, the people who are sharing move toward intelligent activity, with the result of taking action that has a higher potential for effectiveness, spurring on creativity, and helping others serve others. The concept of "effectiveness" is now a shared intent, with the "goodness" of the result perceived by multiple individuals, organizations or countries. [See Chapter 2/Part I; PY15.] Intelligent activity removes forces.[19] [See Chapter 3/Part I; PY3.]

Choose: (1) Strongly Disagree → (2) Disagree → (3) Neutral → (4) Agree → (5) Strongly Agree

Provide rationale/supporting evidence:

4. Cooperation and collaboration reduce forces and enable the free flow of creativity.

Characteristics: Cooperation and collaboration not only reduce forces, helping to bring everyone together heading in a common direction with a shared understanding, but they are also critical to achieving intelligent activity. The reduction of forces allows the free flow of ideas. [See Chapter 3/Part I; PY3.]

Choose: (1) Strongly Disagree → (2) Disagree → (3) Neutral → (4) Agree → (5) Strongly Agree

Provide rationale/supporting evidence:

5. I recognize the power of forces and am able to successfully mitigate or leverage those forces to move forward with new ideas.

Characteristics: Forces are a part of our everyday world. A Force Field Analysis can be used to help identify forces in place that support or work against a solution, issue or problem. It helps illustrate the driving forces that can be reinforced or the restraining forces that can be eliminated or reduced. It also helps identify positive forces that can be strengthened to propel a project forward. [See Chapter 3/Part I; PY3.]

Choose: (1) Strongly Disagree → (2) Disagree → (3) Neutral → (4) Agree → (5) Strongly Agree

Provide rationale/supporting evidence:

6. Humility is not only an excellent learning approach, but it helps reduce forces.

Characteristics: The greatest barriers to learning and change are egotism ("I am right") and arrogance ("I am right, you are wrong, and I'm not listening"). When we respond to others with humility, we take the stance "you are right", *listening* to what is being said and trying to understand their viewpoint. This approach offers greater opportunity for learning, and hearing others' ideas offers greater opportunity for the bisociation of ideas, enabling creativity and supporting innovation. [See Chapter 4/Part I; PY20.]

Choose: (1) Strongly Disagree → (2) Disagree → (3) Neutral → (4) Agree → (5) Strongly Agree

Provide rationale/supporting evidence:

7. I need not be a victim to my unconscious; my conscious self can exercise choice.

Characteristics: In the early part of our lives the personality—working from the unconscious—helps ensure our survival, experience of pleasure and avoidance of pain. As the self develops, we move into the position of making conscious choices. [See Chapter 4/Part I; PY19 and throughout series.]

Choose: (1) Strongly Disagree → (2) Disagree → (3) Neutral → (4) Agree → (5) Strongly Agree

Provide rationale/supporting evidence:

8. The amount of meaning in life is directly related to an individual's level of consciousness.

Characteristics: We never just see some "thing". The mind automatically mixes the external scenes with our own history, feelings and goals (the associative patterning process) to give it context and meaning. In other words, meaning is created out of external events and signals complexed with internal resources (knowledge, beliefs, values, etc.). The more varied and intense your experiences, the greater the potential for growth and meaning. [See Chapter 5/Part I; PY5.]

Choose: (1) Strongly Disagree → (2) Disagree → (3) Neutral → (4) Agree → (5) Strongly Agree

Provide rationale/supporting evidence:

9. I realize that I operate simultaneously on the physical, emotional, mental and spiritual planes, and I seek to integrate all of these perspectives into changing my thoughts and actions.

Characteristics: As we moved through the 20th Century into the 21st Century, there was recognition that people were complex adaptive systems, and that the entangled physical, mental, emotional and spiritual systems could not be separated out from each other but are integral parts of the larger whole. We are holistic beings. [See Chapter 6/Part I; PY13.]

Choose: (1) Strongly Disagree → (2) Disagree → (3) Neutral → (4) Agree → (5) Strongly Agree

Provide rationale/supporting evidence:

10. Awareness, understanding, believing, feeling good, owning and having the knowledge and confidence to act are part of my personal change strategy and growth.

Characteristics: Although change and adaptation is a natural characteristic of the brain, so is the search for safety, security and comfort. To embrace change I need to be aware, understand, believe its truth, feel good about it, feel ownership of it, and be empowered, that is, have the knowledge to change and the courage to act on that knowledge. All of these aspects of us need to be involved in change. [See Chapter 6/Part I; PY5.]

Choose: (1) Strongly Disagree → (2) Disagree → (3) Neutral → (4) Agree → (5) Strongly Agree

Provide rationale/supporting evidence:

PART II: Learning from the Past

11. When we recognize patterns among events, it becomes increasingly easier to connect cause and effect.

Characteristics: The longer the period of time that passes between cause and effect, the more difficult it is to make connections among them. However, as over time layers of connections begin to emerge, there is the ability to develop patterns from these layers. These patterns become formulas, or concepts, that connect the relationships among actions, a higher truth that applies to multiple examples. [See Part II: MOVING FROM THE PAST; PY9.]

Choose: (1) Strongly Disagree → (2) Disagree → (3) Neutral → (4) Agree → (5) Strongly Agree

Provide rationale/supporting evidence:

12. I am aware of a wide variety of change models and methodologies and understand which are most applicable for my purposes.

Characteristics: There are as many models of change as there are people considering change, many overlapping and many applicable only to specific situations. Strategic change programs often fail to deliver because of a lack of alignment between approach and context.

Good theories and the methodologies connected to those theories provide the opportunity for responding to a wide range of situations, allowing us to reflect on possibilities and so better anticipate the results of our actions. [See Chapter 8/Part II.]

Choose: (1) Strongly Disagree → (2) Disagree → (3) Neutral → (4) Agree → (5) Strongly Agree

Provide rationale/supporting evidence:

13. I work to achieve balanced thought, that is, to engage different worldviews and frames of reference when assessing threats and opportunities.

Characteristics: The sign of a mature individual is the ability to hold conflicting world views together at the same time, acting and living, and having life enriched by that capability. This is the ability to see the world globally while simultaneously seeing it as a world of unique individuals. [See Chapter 9/Part II; PY11.]

Choose: (1) Strongly Disagree → (2) Disagree → (3) Neutral → (4) Agree → (5) Strongly Agree

Provide rationale/supporting evidence:

14. I have the courage to think, feel and live my dreams.

Characteristics: Courage is required at all levels of change, from the recognition of choice (and responsibility) to understanding the context, and to taking action in a complex situation. [See Chapter 9/Part II; PY5.]

Choose: (1) Strongly Disagree → (2) Disagree → (3) Neutral → (4) Agree → (5) Strongly Agree

Provide rationale/supporting evidence:

15. I understand the important aspects of my life that provide the foundation of who I am becoming.

Characteristics: Grounded people are confident about who they are, who they are connected to, and where they belong. They understand what value they contribute to others, and have a strong sense of identity. So, how do they know this and achieve a sense of harmony with self? [See Chapter 10/Part II; PY2.]

Choose: (1) Strongly Disagree → (2) Disagree → (3) Neutral → (4) Agree → (5) Strongly Agree

Provide rationale/supporting evidence:

16. I am part of a network of colleagues and friends where trust and openness provide a platform for knowledge sharing.

Characteristics: We are social beings, and learn through our interactions. Cooperation, collaboration and knowledge sharing represent the highest virtues on the physical plane, and form a foundation of trust building. [See Chapter 10/Part II; PY18.]

Choose: (1) Strongly Disagree → (2) Disagree → (3) Neutral → (4) Agree → (5) Strongly Agree

Provide rationale/supporting evidence:

17. Through the sharing of ideas with others, I expand my consciousness and enable the generation of larger ideas.

Characteristics: I share my ideas freely with others and listen carefully to the ideas of others. This is the stuff of creativity. When ideas flow freely there is the opportunity to not only learn but to bisociate those ideas and have new ideas emerge. This is the stuff of innovation. [See Chapter 12/Part II; PY17.]

Choose: (1) Strongly Disagree → (2) Disagree → (3) Neutral → (4) Agree → (5) Strongly Agree

Provide rationale/supporting evidence:

PART III: Learning in the Present

18. When I do not have direct knowledge, I seek trusted sources to achieve my objectives.

Characteristics: Trust is relative. Applicability, accountability and authorization are elements which need to be considered when either giving or receiving trust. [See Chapter 13/Part III.]

Choose: (1) Strongly Disagree → (2) Disagree → (3) Neutral → (4) Agree → (5) Strongly Agree

Provide rationale/supporting evidence:

19. For long-term sustainability, people and organizations (as complex adaptive systems) must change and adapt to co-evolve with their environment.

Characteristics: Complex adaptive systems cannot remain in stasis, but are in a continuoust state of change with high degrees of interdependence. As each element of a complex adaptive system changes, others need to adapt to remain aligned. [See Chapter 14/Part III; PY18.]

Choose: (1) Strongly Disagree → (2) Disagree → (3) Neutral → (4) Agree → (5) Strongly Agree

Provide rationale/supporting evidence:

20. My organization proportionally increases learning activities in order to cope with increasing complexity as we evolve.

Characteristics: Greater levels of learning assist with reducing resistance to change. [See Chapter 14/Part III.]

Choose: (1) Strongly Disagree → (2) Disagree → (3) Neutral → (4) Agree → (5) Strongly Agree

Provide rationale/supporting evidence:

21. We are well prepared to lead complex changes over space and time to create a new future.

Characteristics: People have the ability to adapt to a changing, uncertain and complex environment. [See Chapter 13/Part III; PY21.] Time offers us opportunities. Reflective planning is necessary for iterative enhancement and providing superior outcomes. We leverage time as a critical resource in the planning process. [See Chapter 16/Part III.]

Choose: (1) Strongly Disagree → (2) Disagree → (3) Neutral → (4) Agree → (5) Strongly Agree

Provide rationale/supporting evidence:

22. I effectively construct and leverage stories to influence my Intelligent Social Change Journey.

Characteristics: Our life is a self-constructed story. Stories are proactively collected and shared to co-create thinking about the future. They can be used to ensure a cohesive value system and influence our social development. [See Chapter 17/Part III; PY9.]

Choose: (1) Closed → (2) Somewhat Closed → (3) Neutral → (4) Somewhat Open → (5) Very Open

Choose: (1) Very Uncomfortable → (2) Some Discomfort → (3) Neutral → (4) Somewhat Comfortable → (5) Very Comfortable

Provide rationale/supporting evidence:

23. My thoughts and feelings change the structure of my brain and directly impact my actions.

Characteristics: Energy follows thought. As we are exposed to more diverse and varying thoughts, the brain creates new patterns and strengths of connections and thereby changes its physiological structure. It is also true that the structure of the brain—containing a huge number of networks of neurons—

significantly influences how incoming signals representing new thoughts (that is, patterns composed of networks of neurons) are formed. These new patterns entering the brain associate or connect with patterns already in the brain and impact our actions. [See Chapter 18/Part III; PY1 and throughout.]

Choose: (1) Strongly Disagree → (2) Disagree → (3) Neutral → (4) Agree → (5) Strongly Agree

Provide rationale/supporting evidence:

24. Energy and information flows are aligned to generate optimal performance.

Characteristics: The eight conditions that combine to create the flow experience are: Clear goals; quick feedback; a balance between opportunity and capacity; deepened concentration; being in the present; being in control; an altered sense of time; and the loss of ego. [See Chapter 18/Part III.]

Choose: (1) Closed → (2) Somewhat Closed → (3) Neutral → (4) Somewhat Open → (5) Very Open

Choose: (1) Very Uncomfortable → (2) Some Discomfort → (3) Neutral → (4) Somewhat Comfortable → (5) Very Comfortable

Provide rationale/supporting evidence:

25. I strive to achieve emotional intelligence to fully engage the emotional plane as a guidance system.

Characteristics: Emotional intelligence is the ability to sense, understand, and effectively apply the power and acumen of emotions as a source of human energy, information, connection, and influence. For years, it was widely held that rationality was the way of the executive. Now it is becoming clear that the full spectrum of what it is to be human— including the rational and the emotional parts of the mind—

must be engaged to achieve the best performance in our personal lives and in our organizations. [See Chapter 19/Part III; PY14.]

Choose: (1) Strongly Disagree → (2) Disagree → (3) Neutral → (4) Agree → (5) Strongly Agree

Provide rationale/supporting evidence:

26. The best process for "forgetting" is inattention, and the very best way to avoid attending to some memory is to have a stronger, more significant memory replace it.

Characteristics: We understand that reliving an event embeds those memories deeper into long-term memory, much like purposeful rehearsing, making them more impervious to any possible "forgetting" process. Ultimately, from the mind/brain perspective, that which does not get attention eventually does go away (use it or lose it). [See Chapter 20/Part III; PY6.]

Choose: (1) Strongly Disagree → (2) Disagree → (3) Neutral → (4) Agree → (5) Strongly Agree

Provide rationale/supporting evidence:

27. I recognize that I have—and continue to identify—mental models, and I use this information to assess my responses to challenges and opportunities as they emerge.

Characteristics: Mental models—which represent our beliefs, assumptions and ways of interpreting the outside world—are built up over time and through experience, limiting us to familiar ways of thinking and acting. When new insights conflict with these mental models, they fail to get put into practice. Thus, we must continuously review our perceptions and assumptions of the external world and question our mental models to ensure they are consistent with the current reality. [See Chapter 20/Part III; PY5.]

Choose: (1) Strongly Disagree → (2) Disagree → (3) Neutral → (4) Agree → (5) Strongly Agree

Provide rationale/supporting evidence:

28. The development of knowledge capacities provides the opportunity to move beyond our mental models and expand our frames of reference and worldviews.

Characteristics: While knowledge is the structure we experientially build upon, as we now recognize it is always incomplete and continuously changing. Changing our frame of reference, knowledge capacities provide us unique ways to perceive the world and explore emergent knowledge. [See Chapter 21/Part III.]

Choose: (1) Strongly Disagree → (2) Disagree → (3) Neutral → (4) Agree → (5) Strongly Agree

Provide rationale/supporting evidence:

29. Stimulating behavioral diversity and adaptability builds trust, enhances organizational performance and increases innovation.

Characteristics: Psychometric profilers categorize people into a box. Tools like *The Organizational Zoo* do just the opposite. They remove the box to encourage individual adaptability and cultural diversity. Metaphoric representation of behaviors provides a safe language for behavior conversations. [See Chapter 20/Part III.]

Choose: (1) Strongly Disagree → (2) Disagree → (3) Neutral → (4) Agree → (5) Strongly Agree

Provide rationale/supporting evidence:

PART IV: Co-Creating the Future

30. Our vision can be viewed as a verb, not just a noun.

Characteristics: A vision is not the title of a document. It is an evolving future state that can be achieved through actionable change initiatives. [See Part IV: CO-CREATING THE FUTURE; PY8.]

Choose: (1) Strongly Disagree → (2) Disagree → (3) Neutral → (4) Agree → (5) Strongly Agree

Provide rationale/supporting evidence:

31. In every situation in which I find myself, I take the high moral ground, that is, I choose to do what is best for all those involved both in the short and long term.

Characteristics: As advanced humans, we have become holistic beings who operate from the physical, mental and emotional planes. Because our thoughts and feelings fully integrate into our perceptions of reality and our actions, all of us need to be focused on achieving the best actions. This is the quality of Nobility, representing a virtue of the human, that is, doing the best that can be done at a particular point in time. [See Chapter 22/Part IV; PY7.]

Choose: (1) Strongly Disagree → (2) Disagree → (3) Neutral → (4) Agree → (5) Strongly Agree

Provide rationale/supporting evidence:

32. I am able to expand my empathetic capabilities into conscious compassionate actions.

Characteristics: Conscious compassion is choosing to take action on your feelings of empathy. [See Chapter 22/Part IV and Chapter 31/Part V; PY6.]

Choose: (1) Strongly Disagree → (2) Disagree → (3) Neutral → (4) Agree → (5) Strongly Agree

Provide rationale/supporting evidence:

33. I recognize that I co-create my reality, and I honor the role of others in co-creating their reality.

Characteristics: We are each unique and, collectively and individually, create our own version of the world through thinking, learning, growing and social exchange. Our freedom to think and create offers the opportunity for amazing diversity and infinite possibilities. [See Chapter 23/Part IV; PY8.]

Choose: (1) Strongly Disagree → (2) Disagree → (3) Neutral → (4) Agree → (5) Strongly Agree

Provide rationale/supporting evidence:

34. Discovering truth is more important than being right.

Characteristics: Truth is relative to the amount of information that has been garnered and, like knowledge, is situation dependent and context sensitive. Higher order conceptual thinking has a higher level of truth. [See Chapter 24/Part IV; PY5.] "Being right" is very much related to the ego. In many situations, there is no right or wrong, just choice. By asserting that one is right, it assumes that other approaches are wrong, thus setting up forces. [See Chapters 3 and 4/Part I; PY3.]

Choose: (1) Strongly Disagree → (2) Disagree → (3) Neutral → (4) Agree → (5) Strongly Agree

Provide rationale/supporting evidence:

35. I purposefully focus my attention on thoughts that will move me toward my personal and professional goals.

Characteristics: What we choose to focus on, what comes into our attention, is what we use to make decisions and take actions. When this focus is consistent with our goals, we are providing energy towards achieving those goals. [See Chapter 25/Part IV; PY6.]

Choose: (1) Strongly Disagree → (2) Disagree → (3) Neutral → (4) Agree → (5) Strongly Agree

Provide rationale/supporting evidence:

36. Expectations and setting intent empower my thinking and set the course for the future.

Characteristics: Intention is the source with which we are doing something, the act or instance of mentally and emotionally setting a specific course of action or result, a determination to act in some specific way. Expectation indicates the juncture between where you are and your desire, where you want to be. The creation process of intention and expectation is dynamic and continuous. [See Chapter 25/Part IV; PY6.]

Choose: (1) Strongly Disagree → (2) Disagree → (3) Neutral → (4) Agree → (5) Strongly Agree

Provide rationale/supporting evidence:

37. Conceptual thinking and understanding the theory behind actions supports the discovery of truth.

Characteristics: Through conceptual thinking (the recognition of patterns and relationships among patterns) our higher mental senses tell us when truth is not truth by recognizing forces moving in a different direction. Along with the ability to determine the level of truth of an example, conceptual thinking brings with it an understanding of the relationships among concepts and examples. [See Chapter 24.] Theories reflect high-order patterns, that is, not the facts themselves but rather the basic source of recognition and meaning of the broader patterns, another way of expressing concepts. [See Chapter 26/Part IV; PY6.]

Choose: (1) Strongly Disagree → (2) Disagree → (3) Neutral → (4) Agree → (5) Strongly Agree

Provide rationale/supporting evidence:

38. It is necessary to prepare yourself mentally in order to successfully tap into and act on the intuitional.

Characteristics: Development of the mental faculties is necessary to effectively achieve your Intelligent Social Change Journey. This needs to include a balance of critical thinking, reflection, connecting theory to practice, and understanding relativism and heuristics. By developing our mental faculties, we have the capacity to receive and apply new thoughts and ideas that generate superior outcomes for ourselves and others. [See Chapter 26 and Chapter 28/Part IV; PY13.]

Choose: (1) Strongly Disagree → (2) Disagree → (3) Neutral → (4) Agree → (5) Strongly Agree

Provide rationale/supporting evidence:

39. Intelligent activities are continuously being created by people as, from one thought to the next, there is mental integrity, a consistency in the truth of thought.

Characteristics: Recall that intelligent activity is described as *a perfect state of interaction where intent, purpose, direction, values and expected outcomes are clearly understood and communicated among all parties, reflecting wisdom and achieving a higher truth.* [See Chapter 27/Part IV; PY15.]

Choose: (1) Strongly Disagree → (2) Disagree → (3) Neutral → (4) Agree → (5) Strongly Agree

Provide rationale/supporting evidence:

40. Wisdom occurs when activity matches the choices that are made and structured concepts are intelligently acted upon for the greater good.

Characteristics: Wisdom represents completeness and wholeness of thought. Beyond knowledge, it involves a sense of balance derived from a strong, pervasive moral conviction and provides guidance and obligations that flow from a deep caring for others and profound sense of interdependence. [See Chapter 27/Part IV; PY15.]

Choose: (1) Strongly Disagree → (2) Disagree → (3) Neutral → (4) Agree → (5) Strongly Agree

Provide rationale/supporting evidence:

41. Earned intuition is the result of all of my experiences and the learning from those experiences.

Characteristics: Earned intuition is that part of intuition emerging from the unconscious that is connected to our conscious experiences and discoveries. When we are focused at the conscious mental level, we are always exploring cause and effect and working backwards. This is not the case with the intuition. Something learned many years ago can emerge, when needed, in the blink of an eye. [See Chapter 28/Part IV; PY13.]

Choose: (1) Strongly Disagree → (2) Disagree → (3) Neutral → (4) Agree → (5) Strongly Agree

Provide rationale/supporting evidence:

42. There is a multiplier effect when ideas are shared.

Characteristics: When knowledge is focused inward, *not* shared, it has diminishing value as others continue to connect with the ever-changing and expanding reservoir of knowledge. As we interact with others, we develop a deeper understanding of others and ourselves and an appreciation for diversity. This understanding helps us create without force, embracing a collaborative advantage, that is, gaining the advantage of other's thinking at or above our personal level of thinking, while simultaneously creating in a way that is uniquely ours. [See Chapter 29/Part IV; PY17.]

Choose: (1) Strongly Disagree → (2) Disagree → (3) Neutral → (4) Agree → (5) Strongly Agree

Provide rationale/supporting evidence:

43. We are in the process of preparing to make a creative leap and understand the direction of change this will bring.

Characteristics: The moment of truth has come in which humanity is consciously changing direction and shifting our mind sets to a new level fueled by creativity. We know it is changing the frequency of our energy flows, but remain unaware of the exact forms this will take. The creative leap is a leap of faith and trust. We are comfortable with this uncertainty, although confident the shift will bring about human enhancement. (See Chapter 30/Part IV; PY17.)

Choose: (1) Strongly Disagree → (2) Disagree → (3) Neutral → (4) Agree → (5) Strongly Agree

Provide rationale/supporting evidence:

PART V: Living the Future

44. I recognize that tapping into the intuitional plane is a natural state and that I'm on a return journey to this place of high creativity.

Characteristics: Babies are born connected, to their mothers and families, and to the larger energies surrounding them and within them. This represents Phase 3, which is where we return as adults when we have developed the lower mental mind (logic) and the upper mental mind (conceptual thinking) and deepened our connections with others. [See Introduction to Part V; PY13.]

Choose: (1) Strongly Disagree → (2) Disagree → (3) Neutral → (4) Agree → (5) Strongly Agree

Provide rationale/supporting evidence:

45. As we move into Phase 3, we continue to mature our creativity to become masters of this higher level of co-creating.

Characteristics: Our thinking and behavior remains at the highest level of maturity. The freedom of creativity is the foundation of everything that we do. The Alchemy of our environment is such that science, spirit and consciousness are fully integrated. [See Chapter 31/Part V; PY13.]

Choose: (1) Strongly Disagree → (2) Disagree → (3) Neutral → (4) Agree → (5) Strongly Agree

Provide rationale/supporting evidence:

46. When I achieve inner balance, I am able to cope with a range of external situations that are unbalanced.

Characteristics: Balance provides an inner confidence enabling high function in unpredictable environments. [See Chapter 32/Part V; PY11.]

Choose: (1) Strongly Disagree → (2) Disagree → (3) Neutral → (4) Agree → (5) Strongly Agree

Provide rationale/supporting evidence:

47. As a humanity we are bringing our consciousness back into balance as we engage in the Intelligent Social Change Journey.

Characteristics: In our acceleration of development of the mental faculties, we have focused on the material world and suppressed our inner spiritual senses. Humanity is maturing, and it is time for us to bring all that we are to the table, to reach the full potential of who we are—physical, mental, emotional and spiritual—and bring ourselves into balance. [See Chapter 32/Part V; PY11.]

Choose: (1) Strongly Disagree → (2) Disagree → (3) Neutral → (4) Agree → (5) Strongly Agree

Provide rationale/supporting evidence:

48. I have the ability to engage my senses to perceive beauty in myself and others.

Characteristics: Beauty serves as an accelerator to the expansion of consciousness, enhancing the senses in our body and in others. Simultaneously, when our senses are balanced we are able to perceive greater beauty. [See Chapter 33/Part V; PY1.]

Choose: (1) Strongly Disagree → (2) Disagree → (3) Neutral → (4) Agree → (5) Strongly Agree

Provide rationale/supporting evidence:

49. I recognize the power of beauty and its implications for me and my environment.

Characteristics: Beauty is a short circuit to expanding consciousness, enabling us to circumvent the tedium of everyday life in an instant, and inject feelings of appreciation, love and joy into the essence of our lives. Beauty creates a Oneness within, a balancing of our senses, and, when shared, a Oneness without. Much like the potential effects of a butterfly flapping its wings on the other side of the world, beauty shared can multiply exponentially with wide-spread impact. [See Chapter 33/Part V; PY1.]

Choose: (1) Strongly Disagree → (2) Disagree → (3) Neutral → (4) Agree → (5) Strongly Agree

Provide rationale/supporting evidence:

50. As we move fully into Phase 3 of our creative journey, good character becomes an essential element of our expanded self.

Characteristics: The concept of character represents a quality of goodness and is directly related to growth of the self—individuals and their choices and actions. [See Chapter 34/Part V; PY7.]

Choose: (1) Strongly Disagree → (2) Disagree → (3) Neutral → (4) Agree → (5) Strongly Agree

Provide rationale/supporting evidence:

51. I honor the diversity of others and their potential contributions to the networks of which I am a part.

Characteristics: I am part of a conscious compassionate community that recognizes our connections to each other and that conveys a sense of belonging and Oneness. [See Chapter 34/Part V; PY7.]

Choose: (1) Strongly Disagree → (2) Disagree → (3) Neutral → (4) Agree → (5) Strongly Agree

Provide rationale/supporting evidence:

52. Moving through the Intelligent Social Change Journey has evolved our social maturity to the highest levels of conscious compassion and co-creation.

Characteristics: When we were focused in the Phase 1 relationships of cause and effect, it was important to have sympathy in order to keep people in our formula of change. When we moved into the co-evolving of Phase 2, sympathy was not enough; co-evolving requires empathy, the capacity to put oneself in the shoes of another [see Chapter 14]. Phase 3 requires more, that is, the conscious development of compassion. [See Chapter 35/Part V; PY6.]

Choose: (1) Strongly Disagree → (2) Disagree → (3) Neutral → (4) Agree → (5) Strongly Agree

Provide rationale/supporting evidence:

53. Recognizing the Oneness of all people, I employ empathy and compassion to help me understand diverse viewpoints and how to be of service to humanity.

Characteristics: Our identity as social creatures is hardwired into the structure of our brain. [See Chapter 4.] Empathy, objectively experiencing the inner life of another, is inherent in the functioning of our brain, suggesting that through feelings there is an active link between our own minds and bodies, and the minds and bodies of those around us. [See Chapter 36/Part V; PY6.]

Choose: (1) Strongly Disagree → (2) Disagree → (3) Neutral → (4) Agree → (5) Strongly Agree

Provide rationale/supporting evidence:

54. I realize I am a never-ending fountain of creativity and that there are infinite levels of consciousness awaiting my exploration.

Characteristics: Consciousness is a process. As the self grows and makes good choices, developing virtues and cooperating and collaborating with others through knowledge sharing, so, too, does consciousness expand. As co-creators of our reality engaged in intelligent activity, the only limits are those we set on our selves. [See Chapter 37/Part V; PY22.]

Choose: (1) Strongly Disagree → (2) Disagree → (3) Neutral → (4) Agree → (5) Strongly Agree

Provide rationale/supporting evidence:

55. I am conscious of being conscious, and I am able to pull myself out of the entangled complexity of my past life to start learning and expanding from a simpler place.

Characteristics: In expanded levels of consciousness, out of complexity emerges simplicity, providing a new starting point for our continuing journey, approaching the point of singularity. We are starting to engage in creative co-creation in an environment of punctuated equilibrium. [See Chapter 38/Part V; PY21.]

Choose: (1) Strongly Disagree → (2) Disagree → (3) Neutral → (4) Agree → (5) Strongly Agree

Provide rationale/supporting evidence:

Scoring

Recognizing that average scores are only indicators, nonetheless this learning exercise offers *you* the opportunity to assess *your* personal level of readiness to expand through the three phases of the Intelligent Social Change Journey.

If you average in the neutral zone (level 3) or below, stick with the Phase 1 model, exploring cause-and-effect relationships, and enjoying and applying the kaleidoscope of models (Chapter 8/Part II of the PBC) that have emerged in support of change, each with a differentiated flavor. If you are beyond the half-way mark moving toward level 4, dig deeper into the co-evolving model and make it your own. You are developing deeper relationships with others and ready for more. Once you pass level 4, you are in a field of choice, and have the opportunity to match your change strategy to your desired approach and outcome, tapping into the intuitional field and using your individuated mental faculties to co-create a reality in service to others. All of the 22 volumes of Possibilities that are YOU! can provide clarity for mental, emotional and spiritual expansion.

Take a few minutes to go back and carefully consider your responses. For those responses lower than 3, reflect on what it is about that concept that closes you off or causes some level of discomfort. Quite often, this will be the result of some experience in your history, or a belief or mental model which warrants revisiting. For those responses higher than 3, reflect on how you might use this knowledge on your personal and professional change journey. Can you recall any examples of where this knowledge was used in decision-making or taking action? The more examples you can come up with, the higher the level of truth. (See Chapter 24/Part IV of *The Profundity and Bifurcation of Change*; also, Volume 5, *Truth in Context*, of the *Possibilities that are YOU!* series.)

Remember, there is no right or wrong associated with this journey; rather, it is a journey of *Becoming*. Everyone is a part of this journey at some time, some place, some level. And regardless of where you are, where you choose to be, move into the flow, experience life, and **have fun becoming the co-creator you are.**

In Co-Service, Alex, David, Arthur, Theresa and John

Guide to using this material.

The larger work, *The Profundity and Bifurcation of Change*, has been quite purposefully chunked into five smaller books, referred to as Parts, which are both independent and interdependent. Chunking is a methodology for learning. The way people become experts involves the chunking of ideas and concepts and creating understanding through development of significant patterns useful for identifying opportunities, solving problems and anticipating future behavior within the focused domain of knowledge. Figure 6 shows the relationship of the Parts and their content to the Intelligent Social Change Journey.

Remember: The ISCJ is a journey of expansion, with each Phase building on—and inclusive of—the former Phase as we develop our mental faculties in service to the intuitional, and move closer to intelligent activity. As such, one needs to experience the earlier phases in order to elevate to the upper levels. Life experiences and educational development during these early stages create the foundation and capacity to develop into higher levels of interactions and ways of being.

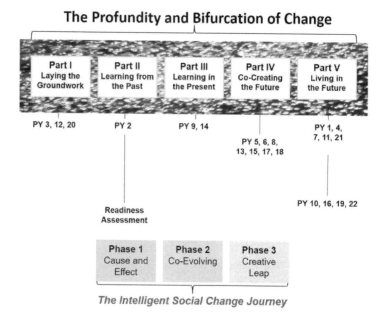

Figure 6. *Relationship of Parts of the larger PBC book, the Phases of the ISCJ, and the 22 little Conscious Look Books.*

While many different ideas about the Intelligent Social Change Journey have been introduced in this little book, each of these ideas is addressed in depth during the course of the five PBC books. Each Part also includes tools, references, insights, reflective questions and cross referencing.

This is a journey, and as such the learning is in the journey, the reflecting on and application of the learning, not in achieving a particular capability or entering the next Phase at a specific point in time. Similar to the deepening of relationships with others, the growth of understanding and expansion of consciousness takes its own time, twisting and curving forwards and backwards until we have learned all we can from one frame of reference, and then jump to another to continue our personal journey.

Still, this is not enough ... in these demanding times this material is just too bulky, too heavy and too time-consuming to read and digest. For this reason, the primary author woke up one morning knowing that many of the key ideas needed to be presented in short bites; thus, the emergence of the 22 little books that are in the *Possibilities that are YOU!* series published by Conscious Look Books. In Figure 6 the volume numbers of these little books are grouped in relationship to the five PBC Parts and the three phases of the Intelligent Social Change Journey. (Volume numbers and respective titles are on page 79.) These powerful key ideas are available in softback format from Amazon.com

Endnotes

[1] Taken from Dunning, J. (2014). Discussion of consciousness via the Internet on December 13, 2017.

[2] See McHale, J. (1977). "Futures Problems or Problems in Futures Studies" in Linstone, H.A. and Simmonds, W.H.C. (Eds.), *Futures Research: New Directions*. Reading, MA: Addison-Wesley Publishing Company, Inc.

[3] See Salk, J. (1973). *The Survival of the Wisest*. New York: Harper & Row.

[4] See Bateson, G. (1972). *Steps to an Ecology of the Mind*. New York: Ballantine.

[5] See Dilts, R. (2003). *From Coach to Awakener*. Capitola, CA: Meta Publications.

[6] See McWhinney, W. (1997). *Paths of Change: Strategic Choices for Organizations and Society*. Thousand Oaks, CA: SAGE Publications, Inc.

[7] See Argyris, C. and Schon, D. (1978). *Organizational Learning: A Theory of Action Perspective*. Reading, MA: Addison-Wesley.

[8] Bateson, 301-305.

[9] Quoted from Berman, M. (1981). *The Reenchantment of the World*. Ithaca, NY: Cornell University Press, 346.

[10] Bateson, 465.

[11] See Fowler, J.W. (1995). *Stages of Faith: The Psychology of Human Development and the Quest for Meaning*. New York: HarperCollins.

[12] See Kohlberg, L. (1981). *Philosophy of Moral Development: Moral Stages and the Idea of Justice*, Harper, San Francisco, CA.

[13] See Hawkins, D.R. (2002). *Power VS Force: The Hidden Determinants of Human Behavior*. Carlsbad, CA: Hay House.

[14] Quoted from de Chardin, P. Teilhard (1959). *The Phenomenon of Man*. St James Palace, London: Collins, 63.

[15] "The Bifurcation" is the last chapter, Chapter 38, in *The Profundity and Bifurcation of Change Part V: Living the Future.* It is also the subject of Volume 21 of the Conscious Look Books *Possibilities that are YOU!* series.

[16] The Self Readiness Assessment was originally published as Chapter 11 in *The Profundity and Bifurcation of Change Part II: Learning from the Past.*

[17] The knowledge we create is both triggered by external events and determined by past experiences and current learning, the process of associative patterning in the mind/brain. Knowledge is the capacity to take effective action.

[18] *Intelligent activity* represents a state of interaction where intent, purpose, direction, values and expected outcomes are clearly understood and communicated among all parties, reflecting wisdom and achieving a higher truth.

[19] The Likert scale, named after its creator, offers a neutral point in the middle and the opportunity for the responder to express negative and positive preferences. We use a five-point scale for this exercise.

The Volumes in
Possibilities that are YOU!

1. Transcendent Beauty
2. Grounding
3. Engaging Forces
4. Conscious Compassion
5. Truth in Context
6. Intention and Attention
7. Living Virtues for Today
8. ME as Co-Creator
9. Connections as Patterns
10. Knowing
11. All Things in Balance
12. The Emerging Self
13. The ERC's of Intuition
14. The Emoting Guidance System
15. Seeking Wisdom
16. Associative Patterning and Attracting
17. The Creative Leap
18. Staying on the Path
19. The Art of Thought Adjusting
20. The Humanness of Humility
21. The Bifurcation
22. Beyond Action

[Available in soft cover from Amazon.com]

The Volumes in

The Profundity and Bifurcation of Change!

Part I: Laying the Groundwork

This book lays the groundwork for the **Intelligent Social Change Journey** (ISCJ), a developmental journey of the body, mind and heart, moving from the heaviness of cause-and-effect linear extrapolations, to the fluidity of co-evolving with our environment, to the lightness of breathing our thought and feelings into reality. Grounded in development of our mental faculties, these are phase changes, each building on and expanding previous learning in our movement toward intelligent activity. As we lay the groundwork, we move through the concepts of change, knowledge, forces, self and consciousness. Then, recognizing that we are holistic beings, we provide a baseline model for individual change from within.

Part II: *Learning from the Past*

Phase 1 of the Intelligent Social Change Journey (ISCJ) is focused on the linear cause-and-effect relationships of logical thinking. Knowledge, situation dependent and context sensitive, is a product of the past. **Phase 1 assumes that for every effect there is an originating cause.** This is where we as a humanity, and as individuals, begin to develop our mental faculties. In this book we explore cause and effect, scan a kaleidoscope of change models, and review the modalities of change. Since change is easier and more fluid when we are grounded, we explore three interpretations of grounding. In preparation for expanding our consciousness, a readiness assessment and sample change agent's strategy are included.

Part III: Learning in the Present

As the world becomes increasingly complex, Phase 2 of the Intelligent Social Change Journey (ISCJ) is focused on **co-evolving with the environment**. This requires a deepening connection to others, moving into empathy. While the NOW is the focus, there is an increasing ability to put together patterns from the past and think conceptually, as well as extrapolate future behaviors. Thus, we look closely at the relationship of time and space, and pattern thinking. We look at the human body as a complex energetic system, exploring the role of emotions as a guidance system, and what happens when we have stuck energy. This book also introduces Knowledge Capacities, different ways of thinking that build capacity for sustainability.

Part IV: Co-Creating the Future

As we move into Phase 3 of the Intelligent Social Change Journey (ISCJ), **we fully embrace our role as co-creator**. We recognize the power of thought and the role of attention and intention in our ever-expanding search for a higher level of truth. Whether we choose to engage it or not, we explore mental discipline as a tool toward expanded consciousness. In preparing ourselves for the creative leap, there are ever-deepening connections with others. We now understand that the mental faculties are in service to the intuitional, preparing us to, and expanding our ability to, act in and on the world, living with conscious compassion and tapping into the intuitional at will.

Part V: Living the Future

We embrace the ancient art and science of Alchemy to **explore the larger shift underway for humanity** and how we can consciously and intentionally speed up evolution to enhance outcomes. In this conversation, we look at balancing and sensing, the harmony of beauty, and virtues for living the future. Conscious compassion, a virtue, is introduced as a state of being connected to morality and good character, inclusive of giving selfless service. We are now ready to refocus our attention on knowledge and consciousness, exploring the new roles these play in our advancement. And all of this—all of our expanding and growth as we move through the Intelligent Social Change journey—is giving a wide freedom of choice as we approach the bifurcation. What will we manifest?

[Available in Kindle and soft cover from Amazon.com]

[Available in PDF from MQIPress.net]